Stories of God's Marine Creatures

Douglas G. Campbell

WESTBOW
P R E S S®
A DIVISION OF THOMAS NELSON
& ZONDERVAN

WestBow Press books may be ordered
through booksellers or by contacting:

WestBow Press
A Division of Thomas Nelson & Zondervan
1663 Liberty Drive
Bloomington, IN 47403
www.westbowpress.com
844-714-3454

Illustrator Joseph Hicks

ISBN: 978-1-6642-1250-3 (sc)
ISBN: 978-1-6642-1249-7 (e)

Print information available on the last page.

WestBow Press rev. date: 12/07/2020

Chapter 1
Atlantic Harbor Seals

I always loved God's creation and enjoyed watching the animals in their habitats. When I hiked through the woods I would hear rabbits thumping their feet, warning of my approach. I would see a fox on the ridge behind me watching my every move. In the 1970's I started working for a state Fish & Wildlife agency and here's some of my interesting adventures. One of my duties working for Fish & Wildlife was capturing sick or injured seals from areas along the ocean shore. As we drove to the site where the seal was reported injured we drove over a narrow steel bridge named the Jamestown Bridge. This bridge was built in the 1940s and history has it that the first person to cross the bridge was with horse and wagon. The driver of the wagon was apprehensive about crossing the bridge because the fog was so thick it appeared the bridge wasn't finished and he would fall into the west passage of the bay. We crossed the bridge and continued on our journey on to Jamestown Island. We turned toward the south side of the island named Beavertail. The name Beavertail was given to this area of the island because the shape of the land that jetted into the ocean. Beavertail was a former navy radio instillation. In the past it had large radio antennas to communicate to other parts of the world before the use of satellites. Two other workers and I would carry a large portable dog carrier to the site of the disabled seal. It would take all three of us to pick up a seal on the beach. Most of the sites were large rocky areas by the shore some with large rock cliffs that touched the ocean. They were not easily reached especially when carrying the dog carrier. We would also carry two canoe paddles with us. You probably are wondering why the canoe paddles. Well each of the two workers would place a canoe paddle one on the left side and one on the right side of the seal or if you are nautical one on the port and one on the starboard. This method was to keep the seal from turning back and biting the person who was picking him up by the tail, that would usually be me. Well I would grasp the seal by the tail and try to get him in the cage. Sometimes they would slide in easily and sometimes it was a fight to the finish. Once in the cage the seal would turn quickly and try to escape. We would quickly slammed the door shut. When carrying the cage from the shore back to the truck you always had to be careful not to place your hands to close to the wire openings on the cage or you could end up with short fingers. The seals we helped were usually Atlantic Harbor Seals and sometimes if you were having a bad day a Harp Seal. Harp seals came down from Canada and had a nasty streak it was like trying to get a Doberman into a cage.

Harbor Seals colors are variable and range from cream to brown. The seals we came in contact with were generally brown. They can weigh up to three hundred pounds but are usually around one hundred pounds. Atlantic Harbor Seals spend much of their time on the ocean's rocky shores and coastal ponds. We would see them sitting on the rocks watching the boats pass by. When the seals were swimming in the water of the bay you couldn't tell if it was a scuba diver or a seal. They can dive up to three hundred feet and stay under water for about thirty minutes. Their favorite food is fish but they also feed on shellfish, crabs and other marine creatures. The seals would be sent to the local aquarium were they would be doctored to health by the Veterinarian and his staff. The seals would be released on isolated beaches when they were healed and healthy. Occasionally we would stop by the aquarium to check on any new creatures that they had acquired such as blue lobsters. While we were in a private area of the aquarium were the public is not invited we saw a California Sea Lion following us around like a dog. The trainer told us not to touch or pet the sea lion. We asked why. The trainer showed us a large scare on her leg and said he bites when he's grumpy. We were happy he wasn't grumpy that day.

Stories of capturing seals were told among the Fish & Wildlife staff. One such story was about two Game Wardens who were sent to rescue a seal on the beach. The seal was alive but not conscious. They determined that they didn't need a cage so they laid the seal in the back of their patrol vehicle. The vehicle they were driving was a Chevrolet Blazer an SUV with an enclosed cab. Suddenly while driving on the way to the Veterinary office the seal woke up and wasn't happy! It started growling and attacking the Wardens. One of the Wardens wrestled with the seal while the other drove fast with lights and siren to the veterinarian's office. Don't worry the seal was fine and oh yes the Wardens too.

Chapter 2

Whales

Whales are God's largest creatures and are the largest mammals on earth. They are becoming more abundant because of the laws that protect them. The local port had boats that shuttled people out to see them in their natural habitat they are called whale watching boats. They would observe large Whales which usually would be Right Whales and smaller whales which were called Pilot Whales. Rarely would other types of whales such as Minke Whales or Sperm Whales were spotted. Right Whales are found in the Atlantic Ocean waters. They are generally black or brown and have some white markings on their chin and belly. The Right Whale can grow to fifty feet in length. Their name comes from colonial days when Whalers referred to the whales as the right whales to hunt because of their slow speed and the fact they swam on the surface of the sea. They feed on small crustaceans which they skim from the water.

Pilot Whales are also seen in these waters and grow to a length of around twenty feet. They are black overall and have an anchor shaped gray patch on their chin and usually have a gray area on their belly. The head looks thick sometimes flattened in front. Pilot Whales feed on squid and fish.

While working with Fish & Wildlife I would occasionally help retrieve dead Whales washed up on the beach. Usually the Whales that washed up on the beach were small Pilot Whales. Well one day while I was working a federal national Marine Fisheries agent showed up at our base. He had received a report of a dead whale washed up on a local state owned swimming beach which was close by. We headed towards the beach in his federal car and discovered a small Pilot Whale washed up on the beach, it was badly decomposed. A curious women on the beach asked what we were doing. The agent said that we were picking up a dead body. The women looked shocked. I quickly spoke up and said that it was a dead whale body. All that remained of the decomposed whale was the head. The federal agent looked at me and said I'm not putting that in my car. I laughed and said don't worry I brought my gloves. I can hang the head outside the passenger door while you drive back to the base. Well it worked and we arrived safely back at the base. The head stayed intact and there was no whale smell in the car. I buried it in a secret burial ground on Fish & Wildlife property. The reason all whales are buried is because they are an endangered species and are protected by federal law. This keeps people from stealing the whale bones for carving's which is called scrimshaw.

Another story I told about whales is when a large forty foot Right Whale was seen dead floating off the coast. The Coast Guard tried towing it out to sea but it was washed back in by the tides. The dead whale floated into the bay and became a hazard to boating. The decision was made to have the whale removed from the bay. The whale was towed to an old naval dock were an old crane was located. The crane lifted the whale on a large eighteen wheel flatbed trailer that belonged to the state's Fish & Wildlife agency. The destination of the whale was to a federal wildlife refuge to be buried in the southern part of the state. The whale was badly rotted and it had a strong odor when it was loaded on the trailer. It was then covered with tarps to reduce the smell and to shield from the public any site of the whale. The truck and the trailer started driving down the road right through the most populated section of town. This section of town is an old fishing village named Wickford. The streets wind through the village of homes built in the 1600s. Rows of old homes and shops line the streets. At the corner of the village is a small park with benches and gardens. At the edge of the road in the park is a sign that reads Wickford formerly Updike Newton. This was the route the truck with the whale was driving. Apparently no one thought the smell would be that strong and everybody in that part of town soon knew how dead whales smelled.

Chapter 3
Birds that Live by the Ocean

Seagulls

There are many species of birds that God has adapted to live by the ocean. They survive in all types of weather conditions and live in habitats that God has created for them. One of the duties I had working for Fish & Wildlife was to check out reports of dead birds. I would receive reports of Mute Swans lying on the sides of roads generally under electric lines. Apparently the swans have no lateral sight that means they can't see electric lines when flying. They hit the lines usually killing them. Mute Swans are large birds four to five feet tall with six to seven foot wingspans. They are white in color with orange bills. They have a black knob at the base of their bill. The Swans are very aggressive to other water fowl and to people. I once observed a swan kill a white farm duck by shaking it by the neck. They are so aggressive that they will scare off all waterfowl in the body of water where they live. The swans build large mound nests at the edge of the water and lay six to eight eggs. They are not native to this area and were brought from Europe to adorn people's estate ponds. The swans have no natural enemies. To reduce their numbers some states have programs to reduce the population by shaking eggs of swans and placing them back in the nest. The swans sit on the nest and the eggs never hatch fooling the swans into thinking the eggs are alright.

As I started walking down the dock to the offshore building on my left I could see a faded white building that sat on a dock about a hundred feet from the shore. On the side of the building there was a faded sign painted on the building that read Shellfish. Boats were tied up and fishermen were unloading bags of shellfish. On my right side was a former oyster house that had been converted to a marina. Boats where lined along its docks and you could hear the clanging sound of the lines on the aluminum masts of the sailboats in the blowing wind. As I walked down the dock towards our offshore building, I stopped and looked and I could see a sea gull sitting on a piling we named Peg Leg Pete. He was a sea gull with one leg. He was a herring gull and apparently his leg was pinched by the ice flows of the harbor cove one cold winter day. Peg Leg was good at standing on the dock pilings leaning into a twenty knot wind without ever moving. You know you can always tell which way the wind is blowing by a sea gull they always face into the wind. The stronger the wind the more the sea gull leans into it. Now this type of herring gull God created is very smart. When looking for food such as hard shell clams they paddle with their little feet in shallow water uncovering the tops of clams. Then with a quick jerk with their beak they snatch the clam from the mud, fly to a height of thirty feet and drop the clam on a hard surface. This could be a flat roof building or a parking lot or sometimes your vehicle.

An adult Herring Gull stands about two foot tall and is white with light gray back and wings. They are scavengers but they will eat anything dead or alive. They are usually seen in landfills or other areas were garbage is dumped. One time during an oil spill many lobsters and crabs washed up on the beach dead. The gulls ate all the oil soaked lobsters and crabs and it didn't hurt one gull. Talk about cast iron stomachs! The Herring Gull is the most common sea gull in this area. There are also Black Back sea gulls. They are larger than Herring Gulls and are white with black backs and wings thus the name Black Back Gull. Their diet is similar to the Herring Gull. Sea gulls generally have no enemies but one day while I was at our Fish & Wildlife lab on the south shore, as I watched over the salt marsh I noticed a Short Eared Owl chasing a sea gull. The sea gull was moving swiftly with the owl in quick pursuit. A few minutes later I noticed the owl returning quickly with a large flock of sea gulls in chase. The sea gulls tried to get the owl but the owl hid in the low brush of the salt marsh. The sea gulls eventually gave up there pursuit and went back to the docks. Other shore birds we dealt with were Common Terns. Terns are about the size of a pigeon they are white with a black cap on its head. Their back and wings are pale gray. The tern's tail is deeply forked.

They nest in areas along the rocky shore or on a pebble beach. One day while I was walking near a tern nesting area the birds started flying close. I was wearing a baseball cap and the terns tried to hit my cap. Remember to always wear a hat when walking near a tern nesting area. There are many types of shorebirds in a salt marsh, one such bird is the Killdeer. The Killdeer is a small bird that lives by the shore or sometimes in gravel banks. They lay their eggs between sand and rocks on the shore. The female will guard the young birds by acting like it has a broken wing to draw away any intruders such as people or dogs.

Another bird seen by the ocean and on coastal ponds is the Osprey. They are a hawk like bird that stands about two feet tall and have a wing span of up to six feet. The birds have a white head with brown on the upper body and white underneath. Ospreys feed on fish and are very good at fishing. They make large nests made of sticks usually on top of electric poles or large trees and occasionally in the masts of fishing boat that has stayed in port to long. One such boat was near our coastal base. The Osprey built a large nest on the mast and wouldn't let anyone near it. The state agency assisted the fisherman by installing a large pole in the nearby salt marsh with a nesting platform on top. They moved the nest to the platform and all was well with the Osprey. The population of Osprey's have increased because of the banning of the pesticide DDT. This pesticide was used until it was banned in the 1960's. It caused the egg shells of the Osprey to become thin, causing them to break.

Well, one day while heading back to our Fish & Wildlife field station traveling on an ocean road I came upon a large amount of small migratory birds laying in the road apparently hit by vehicles. I quickly hopped out of my Fish & Wildlife pickup truck and moved to see if any were alive. Yes, I could see legs kicking and some movement. I dropped the tailgate on the pickup and started placing the little birds on it. I picked up thirty or more birds from the road. After ten to fifteen minutes the birds would wake up, look around and fly off. When all was said and done ninety percent of the birds were saved. After investigating what happened I discovered the birds were eating fermented berries from the Russian Olive bushes and becoming drunk. They couldn't see the cars coming towards them and would be hit. In the Bible it says that God watches over the birds, how true a verse. Other shore birds that we worked with were Cormorants. Cormorants are birds that are great fishers. You would see them sitting on old lighthouses on the bay. They would fly over an area of the bay and dive and catch fish. Cormorants are thirty two inches tall.

They have black slender bodies with a long neck. The Chinese used them for fishing in the past. They would place a ring tightly around the neck of the Cormorant, attached to a rope. The Cormorant would dive in the water and catch a fish, but it could not swallow it because of the tight ring around its neck. The fishermen would pull the Cormorant to the shore or to his boat, remove the fish from the Cormorants mouth and let the bird go to catch another fish. Cormorants stand upright when perched. The Double Crested Cormorant is the most common in southern New England where they spend their winters. They breed from Alaska to Newfoundland south to Mexico. They lay three to four pale chalky blue eggs in a well-made platform stick nest.

Chapter 4
Sharks

Sharks are very interesting creatures God has created. Two of the Fish & Wildlife Biologist I worked with did not like them. We will call Biologist 1, Joe and Biologist 2 Pete. Well Joe went out diving late at night in an area called the Harbor of Refuge. This area is part of a salt pond that is protected from the ocean by large stone walls. The stone walls have two gaps about three hundred feet wide that let boat traffic in and out. On the east side of the Harbor of Refuge there is a large state beach. This beach is used by families with small children because of the small size of the waves. Joe was checking on the local lobster population which apparently is more active at night.

Douglas G. Campbell

While checking out the lobsters something brushed against him in the dark murky water. Joe flashed his underwater flashlight at the object discovering a large nasty looking shark. After seeing the shark he set a new speed record to shore. What type of a shark did Joe see? There are generally two types of sharks seen in these waters, Blue Sharks and White Sharks. Blue Sharks are very slender looking. They grow up to twelve feet and weigh as much as four hundred pounds. Their sides are bright blue, their top is dark blue and their bottoms are white. Blue Sharks have a long snout that's narrowly rounded. They are seen in shallow coastal waters and far out at sea. They are not dangerous to people and feed on small fish that swim in schools. White Sharks are big and nasty. They grow up to twenty one feet long. They look gray or brown on top and dirty white below. There snout is bluntly pointed and their teeth are triangular and serrate. White Sharks live in coastal surface waters and are a great danger to humans. In the Atlantic Ocean they feed on fish and seals. Another story the Biologist's tell about sharks is when Pete was out in his own boat which was about twenty feet long. He was fishing off Montaug PT. New York. Pete had the boat anchored when suddenly a Great White Shark came up next to the boat and stared him in the face. It opened its large mouth and then dove back under water. To say the least Pete pulled the anchor up and got of there as fast as the boat could move. The same Biologist Pete was out fishing some time later about twenty miles offshore in his own boat. The fog bank was rolling in and visibility was around zero. He decided to head for shore using his compass. The boat was not equipped with any radar being a smaller open boat. As the boat moved through the foggy waters Pete suddenly came upon a large steel cable above the water. It appeared to be moving horizontally. At the same time he started to hear waves breaking. What could it be the shore was miles away? Suddenly through the fog he could see the faint outline of a large barge. He pushed hard on the boat throttle moving the boat away from the steel cable. Pete realized he was between the barge and a tug that was towing it and he quickly moved out of its path. He made it back safely to shore and decided to stay clear of the area where barges are towed.

When the summer was coming to a close and Eastern States which is called Springfield Fair was opening I was asked to pick up some sharks from a fisherman in Newport for the exhibit at the fair. I picked the state van and placed a four foot wide by eight long tank in the back of the van and filled it with salt water. As I headed for Newport I arrived at the dock around 10:00 AM. I walked down the dock to the wharf where the fishermen had moored the boat. I asked if they had left the sharks. The fisherman replied that they were in the barrel on the dock. I walked over to the barrel and observed shark tails sticking out of the barrel. I dragged the barrel to the van and started loading the sharks in the van. To my surprise the sharks were larger than I expected. There were two four foot and one five foot blue sharks. I drove back to the Marine Base where large tanks of salt water were set up to accommodate the sharks. I lowered the sharks in the tank, but they remained still. I remembered that the sharks cannot stand still to breath in water they must be continually moving through the water. I placed my hands on their back and pushed them through the water. Their skin was like sandpaper but as I moved them through the water they started to come to life. First the four foot sharks and then the five foot shark. I contacted the office and a hatchery truck was dispatched to the Marine Base. The hatchery truck was filled with salt water. The sharks were loaded in the tank on the hatchery truck and sent to the fair. The sharks were placed in a large salt water tank in the states exhibit building. The sharks were the hit of the fair. There were long lines waiting to observe the sharks probably because the Jaws movies were popular at the time. The sharks were fed live fish that were delivered to the fair every couple days. The fish would be removed from the hatchery tank truck and placed in the exhibits tank. Near the end of the fair a hatchery tank truck was dispatched to the fair with a load of live fish and salt water. The hatchery truck driver did not realize that the water the fish were transported in could not be dumped in the fair tank. Fish apparently produce an acid when they are afraid of their environment. When the fish and the water were dumped in the fairs tank it killed the sharks. The fair exhibit ended up with a dead fish display.

Chapter 5
Leather Back Turtles

Leatherback Turtles

There are many different types of turtles God has created in this region. Fresh water pond turtles such as Painted Turtles or as we call them sun turtles, Spotted Turtles and Snapping Turtles. There are land turtles such as Box Turtles and Wood Turtles. In brackish water where fresh and salt water mix there are Diamond Back Terrapin

Turtles which are becoming rare and are now protected by law. Every so often at Fish & Wildlife we would be called on to investigate a dead turtle washed up on a salt water beach. It was late summer and the air was starting to cool. We were called to a remote beach where a large turtle had washed up there with the high tide. The waves were small and the tide was heading out. The turtle was very large about eight feet long and four feet wide. It was a Leather Back Turtle. They are the largest turtles. Adults weigh between six hundred and sixteen hundred pounds. Their shells are soft and leathery thus the name leather back. Their feet are flippers or paddles and they have no claws. Leather Back Turtles are found in the Atlantic and the Pacific Oceans in open seas and in bays. They are powerful swimmers and swim great distances at sea. They eat jellyfish and sometimes choke on small balloons that land on the surface of the ocean that they mistake for food. The female Leather Back Turtle nests in April to November on the east and west coast of Florida. She lays fifty to one hundred seventy spherical shaped eggs, two to two and a half inches in diameter. They bury their eggs three feet deep and lay eggs several times a year, ten days apart. The Biologists I was working with checked the turtle to determine how the creature had died. The turtle had a large mark on its back that appeared to be from a ships propeller. Leather Back Turtles swim close to the surface of the water and are hit by boats when swimming. Apparently this turtle had the same fate. The field office was contacted and a backhoe was dispatched to bury the turtle on the beach.

Chapter 6
Quahaugs

Quahog Skiff

There are many different types of shellfish that live in salt water in this region that are edible. There are soft shell clams called Steamers, Oysters, Blue Mussels and hard clams which are called Quahaugs or Quahogs. Adult Quahogs have a thick oval shell that's five inches long and four and a half inches high. It can be colored dull gray, brownish or black. Quahogs can be found in sand or mud in salt water from low tide lines to eighty feet deep. The name Quahog was derived from two Narragansett Indian words meaning "dark" or "closed" and "shell". They can remain tightly closed for weeks out of water if refrigerated and are prized for their taste. Small Quahogs are called Little Necks. Medium sized are called Cherry Stones and large Quahogs are called Chowders. Inside the shell of the Quahog is a purple shell lining. The Native Americans used this part of the shell with the purple lining as money which they called Wampum and it was circulated all over the continent.

This is a story about hard shell clams which I will call Quahogs. When I first started working for Fish & Wildlife I was the deckhand on the state's Marine Research Boat. Every year we would have what they call a Quahog Transplant. This is when Shell fisherman dig Quahogs from an area in the bay where the shellfish are abundant but are considered polluted by bacteria. The pollution consists of higher than normal bacteria counts, but no other type of pollutants such as heavy metals, mercury, lead, etc. exist in that area of the bay. The Quahogs are dug out of the water by Shell fishermen and are brought to the larger Fish & Wildlife boat to be weighed. They are then dumped by the Fish & Wildlife staff in the cleaner water when the boat is full of bags of Quahogs.

The Shell fishermen are paid five cents a pound for how many Quahogs they can dig. While the Quahogs remain in the clean water they filter out any bacteria pollutants that are in there bodies. This process takes about three weeks in water that is fifty degrees or higher. In the area close to shore were the Quahogs were dumped, the transplant area will be opened in winter to shell fishing, when the weather and ice prevent the shell fishermen from boating out to the Quahog beds in the middle of the bay. The Quahauger's dug the shellfish with bull rakes. A bull rake is a large curved rake two feet wide with sharp teeth for digging in the bottom of the bay. Attached to the rear of the rake is a large basket that holds the Quahogs from falling back into the water. The handles on the rakes can be as short as ten feet or as long as twenty five feet depending on how deep the water is where you're working.

The Fish and Wildlife transplant started early one morning in late summer. The air was warm and the cove was calm. About fifty shell fishing boats worked in the cove. Most of the shell fishing boats had two men per boat. One man would rake the Quahogs and one would pick and bag them. Picking Quahogs is best described by picking out good Quahogs from dead shells and other debris. There were also Game Wardens watching over the Quahauger's to make sure that none of the shell fishermen would leave without leaving there catch at the waiting Fish and Wildlife boat. The shell fishermen would bring the Quahogs to the Fish and Wildlife boat to have them weighed on an old cast iron Fairbanks scale. They would be paid per pound and the Quahogs would later be dumped in a non-polluted area of the bay by the Fish and Wildlife staff.

While we waited for the Fish and Wildlife deck to be filled with Quahogs we watched a small airplane flying over the bay it appeared to be sky writing. The airplane glided up and down and it started to write first a "P" then an "E", it continued with an "S" everyone looked confused. What was it writing? It continued to write a "P" and an "I". Someone shouted Pespi. What's that? Everyone started to laugh. Apparently the pilot was trying to spell Pepsi and probably became confused or he couldn't spell. As the Game Warden's watched over the cove the fire horn in town started blowing, several Quahogs boats started heading for shore. Game Warden's hurried to shore to stop them but found out they were volunteer firefighters and let them go while they watched over there boats.

As the shell fishermen finished filling their boats with Quahogs, they would dock next to the Fish and Wildlife boat; unload their harvest to be weighed. Every boat that unloaded the Quahogs would have to be searched by Game Wardens or Fish and Wildlife personal, to be certain that no Quahogs would be sneaked out. The reason for this was the water was polluted with bacteria and people could become ill if they ate the shellfish. The little Quahogs called little necks could be sold for a hundred dollars a bushel by the shell fishermen.

The Quahogs boats were about twenty feet in length and most had dog houses on the stern or rear of the boat. A dog house is a small cabin where they can operate the boat without being on the open deck. This protects them from the wind, rain and the waves.

The first boat arrived and the Lt. Game Warden watched over the personal searching boats. I searched the first boat that didn't have a dog house. I noticed in the stern of the boat three plastic battery boxes that hold the battery for starting the outboard engine. I flipped the lid off the first plastic box. I said, why is there so many battery boxes? He replied I don't want to get stuck out in the bay. I flipped the lids of the other two battery boxes and discovered little neck Quahogs in them. The Lt. growled at the Quahauger telling him he would have to appear in court for that violation. The next boat arrived it was quickly unloaded. I jumped down on the deck looking for anything unusual, everything looked normal on deck. I poked my head in the dog house and saw rain gear hanging up. I walked in sliding by the rain gear. I bumped against the rain pants they seemed heavy. I pulled the raincoat away from the pants and noticed little necks sitting in the pants. The legs of the pants were tied at the bottom and the little necks filled the pants up to the waist. I signaled to the Lt. Game Warden what I had found. The Lt. proclaimed there's two bushels of little necks you're going to court, the Quahauger looked stunned. More boats arrived and they were all clean of any violations. It was getting late and the last few boats were arriving and I noticed a boat with three six gallon outboard fuel tanks. I asked the Quahauger why so many fuel tanks. He replied that he didn't want to run out of gas. It seemed strange that he would need that much fuel. I picked up one of the fuel tanks and little necks fell out of the bottom. I picked up the second fuel tank and more little necks fell out. I knew he wasn't running the boat on little necks. I yelled to the Lt. we had another problem. The Lt. Looked at the Quahauger and said you're heading to court. I think the

Lt. Game Warden loved this; he had all these arrests and never had to leave the Fish and Wildlife's boat.

The last of the boats arrived and many Quahogs boats were filled with little necks. Two brothers had dug over four thousand pounds in four hours. The last boat to arrive didn't appear to be hiding anything. The boat was an open boat without a doghouse. It had only one battery box and one fuel tank. The bottom was filled with muddy water. The Lt. starred at the Quahauger and said bail the boat. The Quahauger said he would bail it when he got back to his dock. The Lt. insisted and the Quahauger started bailing and bailing. The tops of little necks started to show and you could see the wooden ribs that lined the bottom of the boat were not the normal four inch size but were eight inch in depth. When the entire boat was bailed, about eight bushel of little necks was removed from the bottom of the boat. The Quahauger had walked on the wooden ribs to give the appearance that the muddy water was only a few inches deep. Well that brought a smile to the Lt. Game Wardens face and you know the rest. As the Fish and Wildlife boat pulled up the anchor we headed out to the transplant bed where we dumped the little necks. You can call it a bank account for Quahaugers and a place for winter harvest.

Chapter 7
Oysters

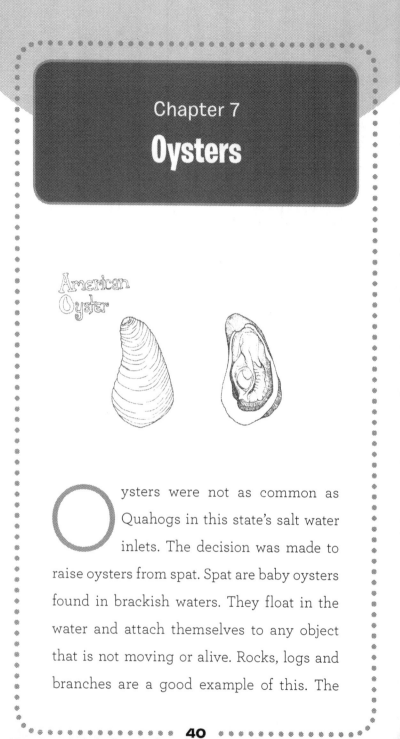

American Oyster

Oysters were not as common as Quahogs in this state's salt water inlets. The decision was made to raise oysters from spat. Spat are baby oysters found in brackish waters. They float in the water and attach themselves to any object that is not moving or alive. Rocks, logs and branches are a good example of this. The states Fish and Wildlife Marine division built floating rafts that measured eight by ten feet in size. From the rafts we hung wires that held strings of bay scallop shells. The wire ran through holes in the center of the bay scallops shells which we drilled by hand. Around forty shells would be strung from each wire. The shells would sit in the water column and the spat, baby oysters would attach themselves to the shells. When the oysters grew to the size of an adult's thumb nail we would remove the strings of shells with oysters attached. We would cut the wire releasing the oysters attached to each scallop shell. This would work exceptionally well because the attached scallop shell would prevent the oysters from sinking in the mud wherever we transplanted them. When God created oysters he gave them the instinct to attach themselves to nonmoving objects thus keeping the population growing.

One sunny day in the fall I was contacted

and told to meet the Lt. Game Warden for a special assignment. Apparently someone had illegally sold oysters to shellfish dealers in our state that were taken from polluted waters which made people ill. My job was to go to the neighboring state and retrieve a bushel of oysters. They would be tested to find out why the people became ill. I drove to the site with the Lt. Game Warden and we met the Game Wardens from the other state. We followed them in our vehicle to the site where the oysters had been taken. The site was next to a large brackish river on a peninsula of land. The land was owned by a company that had abandoned the property. On the property was a house at the end of the road that had been taken over illegally by who knows who. There were attack dogs around the house. The dogs started to attack and while the Game Wardens held the dogs off, I ran down the hill to the river and quickly snatched a bushel of oysters from the water. I wore heavy water proof gloves that slid up to my elbows, just to be on the safe side. The oysters in this area were very abundant. They were so thick on the river bottom they looked like cobble stone. When I finished gathering the oysters I ran up the hill to the waiting vehicles and we quickly left the area. The Lt. Game Warden dropped me off were I had left my Fish and Wildlife truck. I drove to the local college testing lab where the oysters were tested for different types of viruses. No cure for the illness was found and the people eventually became well.

Chapter 8
Blue Mussels

B lue mussels can grow to four inches long and to two inches thick. They are long and look like a round triangle. Blue mussel color range from blue to black. They grow together in dense masses on rocks, pilings and any solid object in salt water between high and low tides. The mussels are edible and are becoming more popular in the United States.

During the warm months of the year I would collect blue mussel's samples to have them tested for red tide contamination. Blue mussels are the best indicator of pollution and toxics in the water. They are used to test for red tide which is called PSP or paralytic shellfish poisoning. There would be different sampling sites around the bay where I would gather the blue mussels, bag them and tag them with location and date of the samples. The health department would send an employee to our field station to retrieve the samples of blue mussels. They would be brought to the lab and tested. Apparently the blue mussels were fed to white mice and lab workers would check them for any reaction. If the mice had a bad reaction more blue mussel samples were requested.

One site in the bay I sampled was directly open to the ocean. I had to climb down a forty foot cliff, slide past poison ivy and work my way to the bottom to a large rocky beach. It had large piles of rocks carved out by the ocean waves. There were a number of tidal pools on the shore. Tidal pools are large pools of salt water on the rocky beach that are filled by the ocean water every time the tide comes back in. In these pools God has provided protection for many types of sea creatures including crabs, sea urchins, and small fish and ocean plants. As I walked down to the ocean I would occasionally see Atlantic Harbor Seals sitting on the large boulders. The mussels were at the edge of the water where the incoming waves broke. I would time the waves and reach in and grab the mussels between each wave.

Sometimes the waves would be small and gentle and other times the waves would be large and dangerous. If ever I had fallen in the water and couldn't get out, no one would have known until the end of the day when I didn't return. We'll God was there protecting me and I never fell in and only got a little wet from the waves.

Chapter 9
Scallops

There were two different types of scallops that we worked with. Bay scallops or Atlantic bay scallops were found in coves in the bay and in salt ponds. Bay scallops adults are about three inches and are almost round. They have ridges on their shells. There colors range from white to gray and sometimes orange in color. Bay scallops have thirty to forty shiny blue eyes on the area between the two shells called the mantle margin. They live in shallow water where there are eelgrass beds; usually the bottom is soft sand or mud.

Sea scallops adults are much larger about eight inches wide. Their shells are round and their shells are smooth with no ridges. Sea scallops are usually white in color with a tinge of yellow on their shells. Their eyes are gray in color and they live in deeper water from fifteen to four hundred feet deep. Both scallops are edible and the scallop's muscle is the only edible part of the shellfish. They are the safest shellfish to eat because the muscle does not pick up any pollution or toxins in the water.

While I was working on the state's research boat we would check the condition of the sea scallop population in the deep water part of the bay. We would load a large metal dredge called a sea scallop dredge on the boat. It was about six feet wide with a chain bag on the back of the dredge to catch the scallops. We would tow the dredge from the boat and drag it across the bottom of the bay. This would scoop the scallops into the chain bag and we would haul up the dredge every ten minutes. Once the scallops were on the deck we would count, measure and check for any dead scallops. The area where we dredged was in about seventy feet of water and was close to a naval base. Almost every time we would dredge for sea scallops we would come up with other debris in our dredge tows.

We would find old navy flashlights, bull horns and other miscellaneous items. Sometimes it was like treasure hunting but most of the items had been damaged by the salt water or the navy. In the 1980's the state marine fisheries section decided to start up a bay scallop hatchery. We built a greenhouse to grow algae to feed the scallops. I helped to build and setup the scallop hatchery by installing a flowing salt water system that supplied the tanks with continuous flowing water. We installed a hot water heater to heat the water around the scallops as they sat in glass dishes to encourage them to spawn. The hatchery worked as planned but was not cost effective because of the small number of scallops that were raised. In nature God has provided a way for scallops to reproduce that's more efficient than what man can do.

Years later Fish & Wildlife marine section decided to buy bay scallops from commercial hatcheries. One hatchery was located in Maine and the scallops were flown in by plane. The other hatchery was in Long Island New York and they were shipped by ferry to the mainland. I would pick up the scallops when they were delivered. We would place them in mesh bags in cages we had built. The cages would be placed around the state in coves and in the bay. The scallops would grow to adults in the cages and spawn in that area's where they were placed. This process worked well but the bay scallops were expensive to purchase.

Lobsters are found in bays and on the open ocean where the bottom is rocky. They can grow as large as thirty-four inches long and nine inches high. A lobster fisherman we knew showed us a lobster trap that was made of heavy wire that had a large hole through the side. It was crushed by a very large lobster that freed itself from the lobster trap before it could be captured. A shellfish house near our marine base also had a large lobster crusher claw on display that was at least a foot long. Lobsters are greenish black on top and have paler color underneath its body. The familiar orange and red color only is seen when the lobsters are cooked. Their legs and claws are red or orange at the tips. Lobsters have two claws, a large heavier claw called a crusher claw which is used for crushing snails and shellfish. The other claw is for tearing apart its prey.

In our salt water tanks we would hold lobsters. The lobsters in the tank would have elastics bands around their claws called banding which would keep the claws closed at all times. This would protect the Lobsters from hurting each other and the Fish & Wildlife staff from being injured or pinched by the claws. Game Wardens would bring in confiscated lobsters to hold in our tanks. They were too short to legally take and held as evidence until the court case was complete. Other lobsters in the tank had their eggs removed illegally by fishermen so the lobster could be sold to seafood dealers and those also were held for evidence. Fishermen would occasionally bring in blue lobsters. Blue lobsters are very rare. One in three million lobsters will be a blue lobster. The reason they are blue are because their bodies do not have any red pigment. Normally lobsters have red and blue pigments in their bodies. The blue lobsters are in different shades of blue from navy blue to royal blue. The marine staff would contact the local marine aquarium and they would pick up the lobsters for public display at their aquarium. The blue lobsters were always a popular display at the aquarium. In our display case at our marine facility we had odd sea creatures. We had a lobster that was half white and half normal color. It looked like someone drew a line down the middle of the lobster and painted white on one side and the other side was normal color. Visitors that saw the lobster thought we were playing a joke on them. Another sea creature we had on display that was found in deep waters was a cross between a crab and a lobster. It had a lobster body, long arms out front with crab claws. The arms measured a foot to eighteen inches long while the body was only six inches long.

The Biologists would tell a story about a former Marine Biologist that was giving a tour of the marine lab to a troop of girl scouts. He was showing the girls a lobster. When he picked it up he was not paying attention were the claws were. The claw of the lobster grabbed him by the chest. His face showed pain and he yelled, grabbed the lobster and threw it. Everyone laughed except the Biologist.

The first year I worked for Fish & Wildlife a nuclear power plant was proposed to be built in an area by the coast. Biologist feared that the warm water discharge from the plant would affect the lobster population in the area. The Biologist did not know if there were any juvenile lobsters called lobster larvae in the area. We were sent to check the area. The forty two foot research boat was used. We equipped the boat with a small mesh net called a bongo net. This net was a rectangular net about six feet long by two and a half feet wide with a small mesh net strung between a metal frame. The boat towed the net back and forth along the shore out to as much as three miles offshore. Every ten minutes we would stop the boat and pull up the net and check for the lobster larvae. The larvae were small and difficult to wash of the nets into buckets. The Biologist would check the buckets and count the lobster larvae. They found a large amount of lobster larvae and used the information to help prevent the nuclear power plant from being built in the area that was environmentally sensitive.

Printed in the United States
By Bookmasters